I0440420

HOW TO SERIES

HOW TO BECOME A SELF EMPLOYED COURIER
DELIVERY DRIVING TO SUCCESS
BY
PHILIP DALE

Copyright©2015 Philip Dale

Followphil Publishing

This manual is simply a guide on how you could make it big in the courier world. But always take professional advice before entering any financial commitments when deciding to become a self employed courier.

CONTENTS

BECOME A SELF EMPLOYED COURIER

Why be a self employed courier?

There are many opportunities to be successful in the delivery business in the UK as either a self employed owner driver or working for one of the major carriers delivering parcels as a same day courier or picking up packages from companies. The courier industry is still thriving with most of the market being dominated by the big international companies. There are also consolidators and others that offer discounts on these companies' services because they are taking thousands of bookings per day so can pass the discounts on to customers. More timed delivery options are being offered for evening deliveries when people are in their homes and this is seen as a growth market due to the boom in Internet shopping.

Almost all businesses use couriers to some extent and it's searching for businesses that have urgent requirements to send small packages, parcels and documents a short distance or a same day service. When building your business plan think about how many jobs you can handle and how you are going to keep your customer informed of the progress of the job. Once the job is completed, you'll need to invoice the customer and collect payment so excellent customer service is key as well as having some form of courier software that can not only keep tabs on the bookings received but also invoice and keep your accounts up to date.

Being your own boss is something many of aspire too. We want to be able to work our own hours however and whenever we like. I mean how many of us have now worked for an employer so long now you look forward to the day you retire rather than just packing it all in. Making that commitment to spread your own wings and take the personal risk is something that at first thought can be quite a scary experience especially if you were to give up quite a good wage. But there are always opportunities out there that will allow you to create a better life for yourself that will allow for more free time to spend how you wish plus the financial gains that come with it. If you do your homework right then self employment courier work will be for you.

There is excellent earning potential, its nothing in this day and age to exceed over £1000 per week undertaking delivery work. As long as you are committed to a bit of hard work identifying the right contact and then being able to deliver first class customer service then the rewards will easily come your way.

Being on the road can also be an enjoyable way to make a living plus the fact it is quite easy to accomplish. All you would be expected to do is take a parcel, whatever size, from one place to another maybe up to 6 times a day and sometime less and if you want to push yourself further than you can make a few more deliveries. Whilst you are driving around the many places you visit you can sing along to your favourite music on your cd or mp3 player and stop off at the many café stops for a relaxing cup of tea and coffee and maybe even interact with other like-minded individuals while you are there. With the steady flow of work plus the financial benefits coming your way you will wonder why you never did it sooner.

The job will also entail you visiting many different locations throughout the country and you will see architectural delights and scenery you never thought you would ever visit. Even when delivering packages to a few faraway places you could book yourself into an overnight hotel thus combining a leisure activity also and of course you are earning all this money at the same time.

Being self-employed is the best thing to do these days, being independent is now the key. More and more people are doing this every day and there is simply no reason why you should not join the many thousands who have taken the plunge and are now getting the rewards that you will clearly get also. All you must consider right now is how you want to run your business, the type of vehicle you want to use and the courier contacts you wish to do work for.

You will be on the whole, a customer facing individual, so there are some aspects that you need to adhere to such as being reasonably smart, maybe you may want to create your own uniform complete with your own logo as a badge. There is not much teamwork involved so own initiative is imperative plus you must want to enjoy your own company as you may be spending many long hours whilst on the road. Always keep a national road A-Z for emergency for navigation, but with sat nav technology, finding your destination has now never been easier. I would also add at this point that you'll need to get to grips with completing invoices and tax returns and such like. But again these are simple exercises as most can be learnt and carried out on a PC or laptop with lots of templates and tutorials available online, but this can be left till last anyway. The point really is if you can drive, use a sat nav and have some reasonable intelligence then you shouldn't have any problem at all becoming a self-employed van driver/courier.

There are many courier companies out there at present and I want to tell you where the best profits are in this line of work and the best way to approach the ideal profit margins. There is currently an enormous amount of parcel delivery work and you can easily access loads of it but you need to decide on what is the best way to consolidate the maximum amount of money for the least amount of work. There are large national parcel companies such as Yodel, TNT and DHL who will gladly accept you as a courier, so long as you have reliable transport and pay your own tax and national insurance. With this criteria met they will normally give you some mainly very local work. You can expect at least 25 drops per day and, depending on the size of the package you deliver, you could be making around 50p to a pound per parcel so sometimes you could earn anything of between £60 and £175 for a 5-day week. So on that basis one can only consider this as part time cash or as some would say a bit of pin money. This may be OK for some but ideally you would be looking to earn a lot more money for doing far fewer drops per day. Also when undertaking multidrops with these larger organisations one would need to consider having a medium to large van such as a Ford Transit at the very least. But this kind of multidrop work blows hot and cold as its not always reliable work due to so many small time couriers competing for this type of pin money. On the other hand if you want to work long hours including weekends, delivering many, many drops both locally and nationally and be on call 7 days a week then multidrop delivering can be somewhat lucrative, maybe £50,000 per annum, especially if the work is coming from a large organization such as DHL.

But for the purposes of being a sole trader with your own vehicle, such as a small van, then without question the largest amount of money can easily be earned by undertaking same day delivery work. Those who operate on a same day delivery basis are able to deliver packages and parcels all over the country and what's more you can even deliver these using your own car or a small light van such as corsa van or Fiesta van. These are sought after vehicles as they are right up there as the most economical. As a courier you would collect a package and transport it to the point of delivery so in effect you could be doing a fair few miles per day but don't let that put you off as the earnings are quite lucrative.

So what would you be delivering? Well it could be anything urgent such as documents or electronic equipment or small items such as gold and jewellery or some urgent hardware/software component part being used by a high tech company. But whatever it is you will be the one being paid to undertake the delivery, as you would already have obtained a soaring reputation for first-rate reliability accompanied with good customer service.

Throughout we will use an example of delivering from your home city of Worcester and delivering to Manchester. In fact when setting up your courier business maybe you will only do delivery runs between these two cities. In other words you will become the specialist courier who others turn to when there are drops to and from these cities. You are offering a standard mileage rate of 90p per mile This would pay around £110 for the one way trip, which is for just over 2 hours work. Then comes an even cleverer bit. You then collect a package from a courier firm in Manchester, at say 70p a mile and deliver it to the company which is either en route back to Worcester or even in your home city itself. For delivering on the home run to Worcester this could pay around £85, you would then have collected around £190 for around 4 hours work and then you get home and relax, knowing you will have several more of these types of courier work during the week. In this small example it shows you are in complete control of your life and not at the wishes and diktats of a large multidrop company where you must make all the drops otherwise you will lose any further work offered, you will also have added extra stress and pressure which will only impact on your health in the long run.

You can take on as much or as less work as you want as a self-employed courier. For extra work with our example of Worcester to Manchester just look at all the towns there are in between these two cities? Just contact any courier firms in these towns and explain to them your destination and if they have any deliveries they would like you to make. Chances are there will be some who will be glad you called. So you can see there will always be some additional opportunities to increase the amount of money you could earn during the normal working day. You also have the potential to negotiate your own mileage rates to maybe at a lower level in order to obtain the courier work as you head back home because as you are going in that direction anyway it's a win-win for everybody concerned. Especially to yourself as these are more welcome profits, which can easily gain you an extra £100 to £200.

So you can see there really is some substantial sums of money to be earned in simply delivering small to medium sized packages to anywhere in the country on route to your destination, to companies on the way to your destination, to companies on the way back to your home town and to companies in your own town. On the other hand you may wish to merely concentrate on local areas only but, as the mileage rates are lower, you may find yourself having to undertake far more multidrop deliveries, which inevitably eat into your precious leisure time, nevertheless there as never been a better time to join the courier bandwagon.

Couriers and multi national parcel carriers are falling over themselves to offer you work. These companies have so much work available that they would soon as pass it to someone like you than have to do it themselves. The reason is simple; it's a question of economics. They wouldn't have to buy a vehicle; they wouldn't have to worry about providing employer liability insurance, national insurance or messing around with tax and PAYE. They simply debit a wage into your account every week or month for the work you undertake on their behalf. So long as you have a vehicle a few trusted references a valid European driving license with a maximum of 6 points and then you're more or less on your way.

As a courier you can be offering an urgent delivery service where something needs to be at a destination as quickly as possible. Some are quite urgent and must be delivered to meet a stringent deadline. Some deliveries may not be so urgent but nevertheless they must still need to get there. These can be items that have to be delivered to the person they are addressed to as opposed to the particular company. This could be legal documents or something similar. In fact as a courier you will be dealing with all manner of different companies and people, which involve, in some cases, highly confidential and sensitive material. Some of the more common users of a courier service are legal companies such as solicitors and law courts, large accountancy offices, publishers whose drafts need to be delivered pronto, architects and design companies, many TV and radio corporations. There are many fashion houses whose drawings and documents need to be shipped quickly. A lot of work will come via small and large sized factories that need to get urgent goods to the trade such as retail establishments and the motor trade. There are also loads of inner city and town Centre offices that desperately need urgent documents to be dispatched quickly for deadlines to be kept. These examples are just the tip of the iceberg so long as you put in the initial homework there can be endless opportunities to be had when it comes to being a self-employed courier.

WHAT DOES COURIER WORK INVOLVE?

So we've looked at the potential now lets to turn to what you, as a courier, actually do. Well as a courier you will be offering a complete A to B delivery service, collecting an item from a companies reception or person and delivering it to its final destination. The collection could be from a reception desk in a small to medium sized factory say, or maybe a solicitor's office or law court. You will be well mannered and smartly presented, as you will be dealing with customers of all levels and experience dealing with a lot of face to face contact. When you arrive at a destination with the package that item will then require a signature as proof of delivery. This is important as the item could be very valuable such as a monetary cheque or an urgent piece of machinery so it must be proved the item was delivered to its correct destination. One things for sure if a business wishes to use your delivery service its because they already know of your ever glowing reputation and will entrust you to deliver this vital item as they know the job will be conducted to a very high professional and courteous standard with speedy delivery as a given, plus it would be undertaken in a safe and lawful way.

A day in the life of a courier could be different on many days of the week. Lets say you are taking an item from Worcester to Manchester with the prospect of a delivery on the return journey home. This could easily pay for more than a days work. However if you get back to Worcester in good time, say early afternoon, you may find you have another delivery to say Bromyard that's not to far from home, plus maybe another delivery on the way back home, say the town of Evesham. Its true to say that many self employed couriers operate like this once they become established meaning they get at least two to three deliveries a day minimum, depending how far you want to travel and the time you wish to allocate to yourself.

In most instances you will be contacted the day before a delivery which could be anytime of the day, so make sure your mobile phone is on and is fully charged. The person contacting you will give you a booking for the following morning. This time of arrangement is ideal as you will know exactly where you will be on that morning this will also give you the opportunity to ring round other courier companies to ask for any additional work to where you are travelling to.

This, suffice to say, is where your earning potential will then significantly increase. Then finally as stated earlier, you can ring some courier companies at the destination you are arriving at and asking them if they have any deliveries for you on your return trip back home.

GETTING STARTED

It would be wise at this stage to begin making your lists of all the courier businesses in your local area. Simply searching for courier companies in Worcester and Manchester simply brings up dozens and dozens of courier firms just like you. Simply enter courier services in the browser and begin taking the phone numbers and email addresses of all those that appear.

Now its fair to say that nearly all these companies have lists of the self employed couriers they use and trust. But that doesn't mean you wont get a look in, far from it. There is so much courier work out there that they will simply bite your hand off for you to get their stuff delivered. So simply get on their company courier list as quickly as possible. Believe me there is plenty of delivery work but it doesn't mean you will get work at the drop of a hat; remember there are others they use regularly. But at some stage in the near future they almost certainly will contact you. So get yourself listed with as many courier firms as you can and as soon as one company uses you then this could very well snowball to regular work. Also one of the things that courier companies like will be your flexibility on mileage prices. So if you are prepared to offer a reduced delivery price, initially to undertake the first drop with them, then this could certainly enhance your chances of them giving you the order to deliver.

Of course courier companies cant give you work if they don't know you exist. So it's now time to become more proactive and to let the courier companies know that you are out there. After you have got your courier list its time to begin writing out introductory letters to them in order to introduce yourself as a reliable courier service. The points you need to get across are that you are available to offer your services as a self employed courier service, including the type of vehicle you use and details of the hours available, although that bit is optional as I would be happy to work any hours initially in order to get the work and to get recognized as a reliable courier. Perhaps later you may want to stipulate your hours of work in which case you may want to offer 24-hour cover but then later change to a more normal 9-5 if you wish.

The outlay in postage for sending out introductory letters will certainly be offset by getting probably your first delivery order. Another cheaper method would be to get their email addresses and send all the relevant information in this format. As an example of your intro letter or email it could resemble something like this;

TO BE READ BY THE OPERATIONS MANAGER mark your letter private and confidential

I am writing this quick note to inform you of my services as a self-employed courier/delivery driver.

I am currently available to undertake deliveries from your company to any part of the UK 7 days a week and usually at very short notice. I am smart and reliable with a clean and tidy van (stipulate here the type of van and age of the vehicle) The van is fully insured for courier use a copy of which can be seen if you so wish by fax or posted to you or by sight. I also have employer liability insurance, which again you may have sight to if required. I can also provide you with written character references if you so wish.

I provide a professional service including first-rate customer service. I have excellent knowledge of the courier business and I know reliability to customers is key.

I therefore ask if it would be possible for you to call me so that I can see you at your earliest convenience so I can discuss your requirements for delivery expectations and the service I can provide for you.

I appreciate you taking the opportunity to read this letter/email and would look forward to hearing from you very soon

Best Regards

Your Name signed in your own hand if it's a letter.

Self employed courier (or name of your courier company if you have one)

Obviously this letter is simply a guide only so change it to suit you in order to get the best impact. There are many examples of similar letters online. Just browse for introductory letters on Google for instance.

Next thing is to get some business cards printed. These should simply state your name, job title i.e. courier services, Reliable service offered
Available for any kind of delivery work
Your phone number (obviously mobile number)

You can get yourself a few hundred business cards these days at reasonable prices. There are even business card printing machines in shopping centres. But suffice to say there are many online companies who will provide you with a good deal on these, in fact you could even print your own if you have the right software. Again search online for the best prices.

FOLLOWING UP EMAILS AND LETTERS

As I mentioned earlier contact the entire courier services in your area. After about 10 days you should effectively make a follow up telephone call in order to ensure the company has received your introductory letter or the email has been read. With an email there should be no reason why the company would not have replied but nevertheless follow up on this also if no reply has been received. Hopefully if it's a letter it should have been delivered to the operations manager, so ask to speak to that person to confirm they have received it.

Again try not to be overly concerned if you are not contacted with work straight away, as I said, they use many other couriers but there is always work for more couriers. It could take up to as long as a month before they phone you with work, so long as you have followed up your letter/email by phoning or emailing them there is simply no reason why they shouldn't give you an opportunity.

Also Its not unusual for these companies to give you work on the same day they receive your letter or email but again others may take a few weeks but the beauty of it is that once they use you and you carry out the work professionally and above all reliably, then you will find yourself receiving regular work. As a further follow up, contact those companies who have not yet contacted you after say a further month just to remind them you still exist and available and ready for any delivery work they have on offer.

STUFF YOU WILL NEED

As a sole trader you will need to have either an invoice book or an online invoice package that will allow you to print off an invoice although a book of invoices is just as good. But if you are savvy with excel and databases then you can easily keep track of the customers you deal with, and easily print off the required invoice. Although, again searching on Google, will easily uncover invoice templates you can use free of charge.

You will also need to keep track of your accounts by undertaking some simple bookkeeping either in a ledger of some sort or on your computer. Its not something you need to get concerned over initially, getting your sole trader business up and running is the priority, but later on you will need to start keeping a running check of your expenses. If you look online you will easily find some basic accounting articles that will show you how to complete your ingoing's and outgoings for computers or in a simple ledger which you can purchase from any stationer.

Back in the day the only way to get around in a car or van was with a road atlas and a local A-Z for each locality you visited and even then trying to locate the road on an A-Z was never simple, that's why we were always having to wind down the window asking for directions and then the person usually giving you the completely wrong directions anyway So the answer of course is a satnav, tom tom seem to be the most popular at present especially those that offer free speed camera alerts. No doubt as a courier you need to get to your destinations as quickly as possible so this type of sat nav would prove very useful.

Then there is the smartphone. Any will do but your mobile package should contain unlimited Internet access and unlimited call time. These types of packages are getting cheaper so shop around for the best deal. Then for your vehicle you would need to equip it with Bluetooth answering equipment as you will be making and receiving calls whilst you are on the move. A mobile phone holder is also useful as you may have to answer many calls whilst driving, lots of holders are available on eBay.

Being a professional courier you will require an attitude of courtesy. Unfortunately there could be many instances when you will be unavoidably delayed due to traffic hold ups, in which case it is only common courtesy to contact the company you are delivering to inform them of your delay. Therefore it's always a good idea to have a phone charger within the vehicle in case your mobile runs low on power. When you are pricing your delivery on per mile travelled when answering a call from a prospective client then you can use the internet on your mobile to calculate the distance from the companies delivery point to the destination so a price can then be negotiated. Google maps can calculate the mileage very easily. To get an idea of what other courier companies are currently charging for delivery you may get an idea by visiting their web site when you're doing a spot of research homework in your spare time. If this information is not available then a simple call to them asking how much would it cost for a same day delivery to some company you are planning to visit, this will give you at least some idea as to what other companies are currently charging.

Your physical appearance is also of most importance. You will need to look the part and that means appearing smart in appearance with clean clothing. Nothing beats that professional image. If you take pride in yourself then you immediately portray to others that you take pride in your business. There will be many occasions when you will be delivering packages to conference centres and other highly professional organisations and the last thing they wish to see is some scruffy, unkempt individual standing at reception. When word gets back to the company who hired you I doubt they would want to use you again, so impressions matter as you will be representing the courier firm that sent you originally as well as the company who was the sender of the package.

You will also need a delivery note to confirm the item as been delivered. Again these are fairly straightforward templates, you can obtain free delivery note templates online or you can create your own using excel software. You can also buy delivery note books from stationers. On delivering the package identify the addressee and get their signature on the delivery note. The delivery note itself should display the basic information; the date, collection address (the company you collected the item from) the delivery address, a column for the goods description or its consignment order. Then below this you will get the customer to sign and print their name together with date and time of delivery and the number of items delivered to that person.

A home printer with a fax and copier/scanner incorporated is also going to be very useful as you can photocopy all delivery notes and invoices. So create your own filing system to keep check of all your paperwork for self-reference and tax purposes. The original delivery note can be then posted, faxed or returned in person to the original company whose parcel you've delivered to show proof of delivery to the assigned address. But all courier companies who you will work for will explain to you exactly how their method of proof of delivery works for them, so don't get concerned at this stage as this is all explained to you by the courier companies themselves.

In fact when you have undertaken several drops for these companies you may very well be issued with a hand held mobile device where you can simply scan the barcode on the package, which brings up the address on the device. The customer uses the electronic pen to sign for the goods on the small screen. On return to the depot the information is uploaded to their computer and shows all signed for deliveries. Also this can be done using your own computer at home in which case the delivery company will give you access to the software for you to upload your deliveries. Again the courier companies will show how all this is undertaken if that is their method of recording deliveries. After the uploads you simply put the mobile device on charge.

POTENTIAL EARNINGS

Anyway the reason anyone wants to go self-employed is because of the independence, no bossy individuals telling you what to do and the potential to make good money. As I stated earlier there is now more potential than ever to make serious money as a courier. Companies are always on the look out for self-employed, reliable, smart individuals with their own transport who they can do business with. There are parcels, boxes, packages in all shapes and sizes, all waiting to be delivered with many courier firms fully stretched and they will always welcome new couriers on their books and that's a fact. So earnings of well over a £1000 can be achievable. So lets see how this can be done.

Most courier companies will pay by the mile and its up to you what your charge will be. Sometimes the courier company themselves will tell you what they are prepared to pay for you to deliver a package. Some vehicles need more maintenance costs plus fuel may be dearer based on your vehicle. As a rule of thumb if you have a small van then the charge is around 85p a mile, a transit van about £1.10 per mile and a larger van say around £1.25 per mile, If its a car then that's around 85p per mile.

So a Worcester to Manchester trip in a transit would be around £125 to £130 for a one-way delivery. Depending on where the courier company is sending you then you may be collecting from them to bring back to your home location so an extra 25-30% is then added to the total cost for the journey there and back. Plus don't forget the price per mile can be upped if the delivery job is outside of the normal business hours say an extra 30%. So that one-way journey to Manchester could now be around £160.

To obtain extra earnings you should ideally be contacting all the local couriers on your contact list. So before you collect your delivery from the courier company you should hopefully have another local courier company you will be visiting so they can use you to deliver to an address to Manchester (as our example) or you will be delivering to another company on the way there. This effectively is doubling your money and its not even putting you out as you are heading that way anyway. And as you are already going that way then you can negotiate a reduced rate so that the courier company will very likely use you. They would obviously prefer to give you the work at the reduced rate than pay someone the full amount. So however way you look at it you will gain increased profits without increasing your mileage and the company does ok out of it because they have got the delivery done at a lot cheaper rate, which increases their profits also.

So lets say you are now in Manchester and have delivered the packages. As I've said you may already have some package to bring back on your return journey but there is nothing stopping you from contacting the local courier companies in the Manchester area. As I've stated earlier doing your homework is important you can research the local courier companies in Manchester whilst at home and put their contact numbers in your smartphone. So in Manchester you could ring around and let them know where you are going and ask them for some return work. Your journey up to Manchester as already been factored in so getting some extra work while driving back home will increase your earnings quite a bit. Again as you are on the return journey you can always offer the courier company a reduced rate in order to get the business, so instead of £1.25 per mile you could opt for say 90p they would probably snap your hand off. This will be extra profit to you as you are on the way back home anyway.

One of the other benefits of being self employed is you can set your own times and days when you want to work. In many ways this can be equally applied to courier work. You can make a decision as to whether you want to deliver or not. In these instances you are simply stating to a company that you cannot deliver today due to other commitments. But that kind of reasoning may be a little way off in the early days, as you want to get yourself established amongst courier companies, as they will quickly recognize you as someone they can trust to get the job done. So when you do become noticed as a reliable and professional courier you may start to get some contract work. This type of work is when you don't necessarily get to choose your own hours or days of work. The contract you agree with will be offering you set times and days of the week to make the deliveries. This could involve drops every day of the week or maybe a couple of deliveries per week. It's entirely up to you if you decide to enter into contracts with delivery companies. It will impact on your free time though but the advantage is you get established and regular work meaning their will always be money going into your bank account. Another reason to consider contract work, if it is offered, is if there isn't any other regular courier work coming your way, but in my experience that should never happen.

Using the Internet is a great tool to always getting courier work. Take a look for instance at COURIER EXCHANGE. You will need to get yourself registered with the site and there is a fee to join and in return you will be sent a text message of the work available wherever you are heading. In our example of Worcester to Manchester you log on to this site to see what other delivery drops are available en route to and from your destination. If there is some delivery work available you can discuss the price with the company by getting in touch with them direct.

Another similar site is MTVAN. Again they have regular work advertised which, when registered with the site after paying a membership fee, you will have access to a good database of courier work covering all areas. You will more than likely find delivery drops that will be suitable for you as you head up to say Manchester from Worcester and back again. You can also advertise your return journeys on these sites, meaning you are arriving in Manchester from Worcester and are looking for return work homeward bound. You will find that all courier companies subscribe to these sites so there is always urgent and regular delivery drops available.

But remember these are good tools to use but shouldn't be considered as your main revenue streams as there may not always be drops available. Your main objective is to list as many courier companies as you can find and use them. Then you phone them to let them know you are available for delivery drops and the chances are work will come your way.

INVOICING COURIER COMPANIES

Whenever you undertake any delivery for a company you need to establish their payment terms. Some companies have been known to pay cash in hand on the day but most prefer to pay you on a monthly basis for all work undertaken although some also pay weekly. Some companies pay you by cheque but the norm is payment straight into your bank account. The bank account route is usually when you are getting regular work or contract work from a delivery company so it makes sense for them to have your business bank details for them to pay into it. Otherwise the payments will generally be by cheque with most companies you do work for.

You will require an invoice for all work you do. The invoice will tell the delivery company the work you have done A typical example is the invoice showing your name and the invoice number at the top. Next it will display who the company you did the work for and the date and description of the work undertaken. Example being let's say, 3 boxes of photographic equipment delivered to J.Bloggs, Manchester - mileage 135 miles. At the bottom of the invoice will show total cost plus VAT, a grand total and a BALANCE DUE being the last figure. The balance due is the amount you are charging the courier company for the work they gave you to deliver, after deducting all other expenses.

The Internet is a great source to find all sorts of invoice templates or you can purchase an invoice book from any stationers. Also attach any delivery notes you have for the job you undertook so the courier company can see that the delivery was completed. Again in some instances courier companies who use you regularly will issue you with a hand held mobile device that has the delivery jobs on the software and it shows the signature of the person who took delivery, so a delivery note would not be required. But initially your work will mainly involve getting a signature on a delivery note at the point of delivery and attaching this to your invoice when you are claiming the balance for the job done. It will be quite a rarity to come across many problems with late or even non payments from companies as they rely heavily on self employed couriers and if you don't get paid then word easily gets around that this particular courier company is a bad payer and pretty soon they wont be able to get drivers to do work for them. Reputation is everything both as a courier company and as a delivery driver like you.

PAYING YOUR TAX AND VAT

When you become self employed it is your responsibility to inform the tax authorities what you are doing. Generally most want to get up and running as quickly as possible in order to get established. But with the threat of fines and such like by the Inland Revenue you will need to let them know sooner rather than later. The easiest way to get registered with the Inland Revenue is to do it online.

Keeping check of your own accounts is fairly straightforward. You are simply keeping a register of all work you do and the amount charged for each job. But as a courier there are many tax relief benefits to be taken into consideration when working out how much tax to pay at the end of a tax year. For instance you can claim for the use of your mobile phone and for any bills relating to a room in your house you use as an office in the course of your courier work, such as heating, lighting and stationary as its all related to your job. There is also tax relief for your vehicle especially in the first year. You can find what to claim for and how to claim for these types of expenditure by exploring online or alternatively, if you can afford it initially, contact an accountant who will easily sort out your tax bills for you. You will be surprised what you can claim for when you become a self employed courier. Registering for VAT is not something that you will be doing any time soon. But once you reach the threshold of how much gross earnings you receive in a year than that will be the time to inform revenue and customs. The Inland Revenue site will give you more information about what the threshold is.

Put simply you need to keep a running check of all your expenses relating to the running of your business. As a sole trader there will be many items you will need to keep an eye on which is anything from the fuel you pay for to the printer cartridge for your printer. So make sure you get a receipt for everything that is related to your business and that includes receipts at the petrol garages.

A good thing also is to have a bank account solely for business use. There may be a small charge by your bank to service this but you will find it more than useful. Then a ledger of some kind from a stationer where you can enter money coming in from courier companies and entering monies paid out for use in your business. Without going in to too much detail a ledger will self explain how to complete it. Otherwise I refer you the many YouTube clips online, which shows how easy it is to complete a ledger of incomings and outgoings.

You can then forward this information together with all receipts to your tax accountant at the end of the tax year if you wish to use one, so they can calculate any tax relief and other benefits, in order to reach a final figure for tax revenue. Otherwise you can work this out for yourself and send the amount together with your tax return form. But remember to use a filing system to keep all receipts and other business related documents safe in case they may need to be referred to at a later date.

WHAT TYPE OF VEHICLE TO USE

Now, we have mainly talked about your vehicle as a van. There are several types of van out there. The most economical tend to be the car like Fiesta van and Corsa van otherwise a small van such as ford or Fiat. Many of these car companies manufacture small to medium type vans and it will come down to your preference and what you can afford. For first time couriers who are just starting out in the delivery business will use the small van, as we are mainly dealing with same day deliveries, which don't tend to be very large packages. When you become more established and courier companies recognize you as reliable and dependable you may get some contract work of the type I mentioned earlier. In which case maybe a medium sized van could be more appropriate. Even better the company may even lease you a vehicle for this purpose but I've found that to be rare. They expect you to provide your own vehicle. Incidentally we have mentioned a van but there's nothing wrong in a large car such as an estate and with the seats folded down, can accommodate quite large loads.

If your only vehicle initially is a car you could still approach courier companies by writing to them to offer your services to deliver packages. In this way you will begin to get a feel of what the type of work is like and can then decide if its for you or not. This probably is a better way to go about it without shelling out for a van, otherwise you could end up committing yourself to a lease, if you decide to go down that route when setting up your courier business, and if your earnings expectations haven't been reached you may find yourself out of pocket.

Once you have made your first few deliveries you may then decide to purchase a small van by means of a loan or maybe a lease. When it comes to a small van ensure its been well maintained if used as well as economical which generally means a diesel van.

Incidentally you may get some Government backing to set up your business. There may grants in your area for self-starter packages or agreements with banks with low interest loans. To find out if you're eligible for financial help then contact the Gov.Uk site about starting your own business.

Obviously keeping running costs down with the van is important as the vehicle will soon eat into your profits and if its off the road for any length of time due to repairs and other maintenance aspects it can seriously cost you. A new van would be the ideal but of course that could be out of your reach in which case a good low mileage economical diesel van is your next option, one that has been well looked after. Diesel vans, if well maintained, can be expected to drive as far as the moon, which is around 240,000 miles, but many vans can well exceed 300,000. Many courier firms prefer it if you have a van, but as stated before; many courier firms are desperate for drivers so a larger car may not necessarily go against you if that is your only vehicle available to you.

WHERE TO GET THE BEST INSURANCE QUOTES

When staring your courier business you will need to get the vehicle taxed and insured. Tax discs no longer need to be displayed so they can now be purchased online through the DVLA. There is several van insurance comparison sites available online so use these to get the best deal possible. There tends not to be any brand loyalty with insurance companies these days. They tend to sign you up with a taster deal and then 12 months later you receive a letter that informs you the insurance premium as dramatically increased. In which case check the comparison sites once more and get a better deal. You will find that you will have a different insurance company each year, but who cares its about getting the best deal for you. But again this depends on the type of van insurance you need as in many cases van insurance is more specialist, as it requires information regarding what you are delivering.

Although you can get cheaper insurance rates it doesn't necessarily mean it's better than someone who is charging more. But you have to ask yourself do I need all the extras such as roadside recovery or personal injury cover etc. Courier insurance can be specialist however, as not only the vehicle is to be insured, but goods also need to be covered for loss and damage. In my experience a lot of courier companies who want to use you will want you to have loss and damage cover, although it is optional. This extra cover will cost more but ultimately it will get you more delivery work. Public liability insurance is also something to consider as this can cover you for any expensive legal bills if they arise such as an accident but this is optional so its your choice how you wish to approach this when setting up your business.

AND FINALLY...

There is big money to be made as a self-employed courier. Take a look at all the courier companies in the areas where you wish to deliver to and you will easily find a fair few. To begin your business you are ideally looking to contact all the local courier companies perhaps within a 20 mile radius. After sending out your contact letter and then following it up with a phone call or email it wont be long before your first delivery will come through. Make sure your smartphone is on and fully charged, as you never know when that call will happen, but happen it will.

The courier company will ask you to pop round to their company to collect the package. On the way you may want to be phoning other courier companies nearby explaining where you are heading and do they have any work to deliver in the same vicinity as you are heading to. When you get to the courier you will discuss payment terms if not already done so by phone and the invoice and delivery note system will be discussed also. Make sure you have your sat nav up and running plus phone charger, plus your delivery notes for signing when you get to the point of delivery.

Once you reach your destination you can spend a few minutes ringing around the couriers in that location and asking if they have any drops for you to deliver on your return journey home, remember you can offer a discounted rate for return journeys. Once you have done a few of these types of deliveries then sign up and register with online courier sites such as courier exchange and mtvan. On here you can see what work is available for you, as well as advertising your services on these sites so courier companies can phone you with the offer of extra work.

Word of mouth is generally your best advertising. So be professional and courteous at all times. Look smart and neatly dressed; provide yourself with your own uniform if you wish with your own LOGO displayed on your uniform and stationary. Eventually you may want to give your van some signage with your business name on the side with your mobile number, again this could also attract passing trade who may wish to use your services. There are may other ways of advertising your courier business such as newspapers and trade magazines as well as issuing business cards to as may people as possible who could be interested in using your services.

But all in all if you start out right and do your homework there is simply no reason whatsoever not to be earning a very good weekly salary indeed, which will then lead you to think 'why didn't I do this sooner'? Before you know it you may one day very well end up running your own small courier business employing other drivers to work for you, while you sit behind the desk taking phone calls and drumming up more business for your company. Or alternatively you may decide to go out and play a few rounds of golf instead whilst your secretary does the graft on your behalf. There really is no end to the potential, so come on, what are you waiting for?

GOOD LUCK AND I HOPE YOUE ACHIEVE THE SUCCESS YOU DESERVE. PHIL